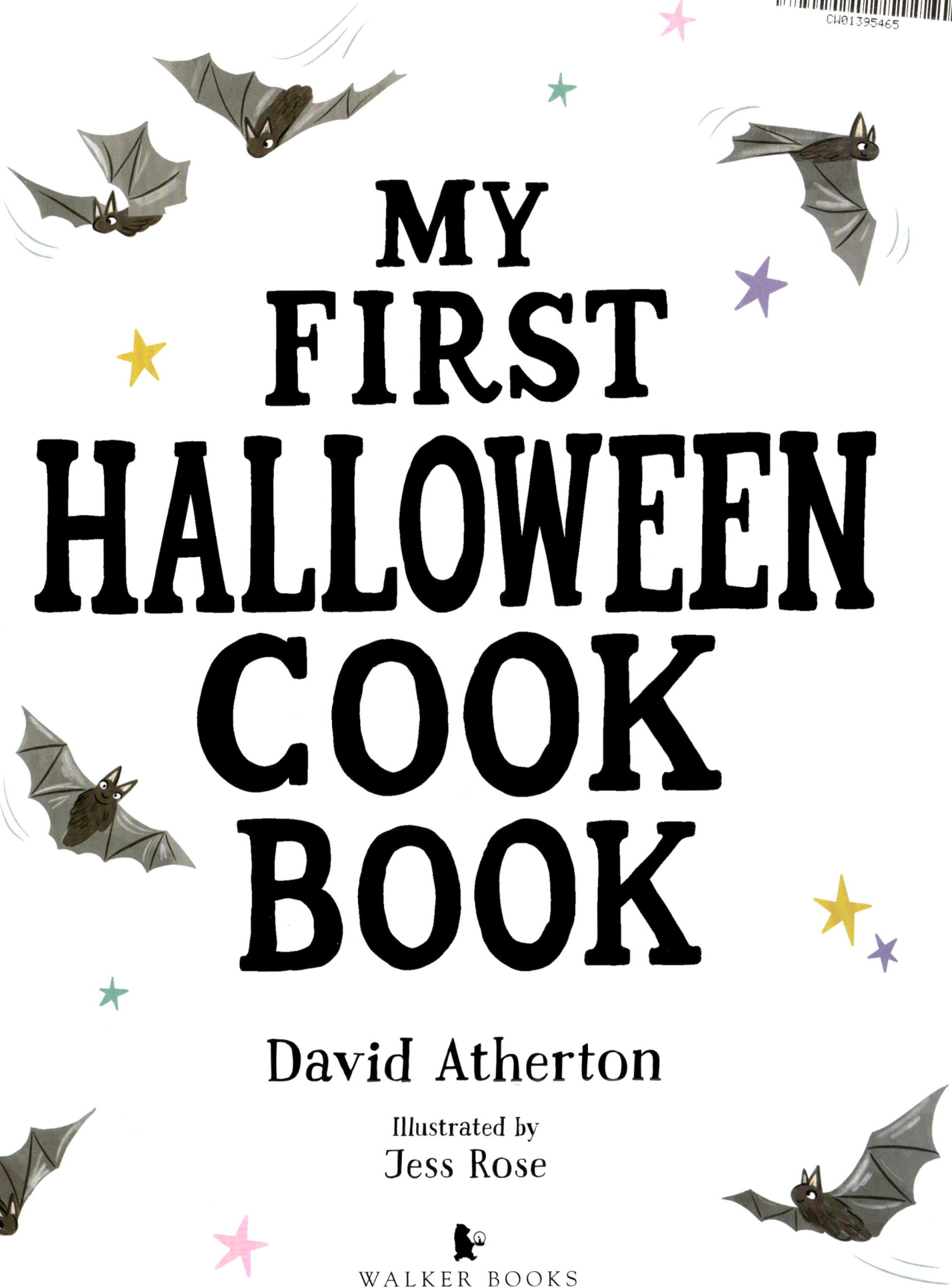

MY FIRST HALLOWEEN COOK BOOK

David Atherton

Illustrated by
Jess Rose

WALKER BOOKS
AND SUBSIDIARIES
LONDON · BOSTON · SYDNEY · AUCKLAND

I want to give a massive shout-out to the Walker team. There are so many people behind a book, but a special thank you to Denise, who started it all; Sarah, my partner in crime; and Jamie, who realizes the vision (literally).

D.A.

To my beautiful children, who share my love of Halloween and bring a lot of laughter to our home.

J.R.

First published 2025 by Walker Books Ltd, 87 Vauxhall Walk, London SE11 5HJ
10 9 8 7 6 5 4 3 2 1
Text © 2025 Nomadbaker Ltd Illustrations © 2025 Jess Rose
The right of David Atherton and Jess Rose to be identified as author and illustrator respectively of this work has been asserted in accordance with the Copyright, Designs and Patents Act 1988
EU Authorized Representative: HackettFlynn Ltd, 36 Cloch Choirneal, Balrothery, Co. Dublin, K32 C942, Ireland. EU@walkerpublishinggroup.com
This book has been typeset in Alice and Mrs Ant
Printed in China
British Library Cataloguing in Publication Data: a catalogue record for this book is available from the British Library
ISBN 978-1-5295-2481-9 www.walker.co.uk

All recipes are for informational and/or entertainment purposes only; please check all ingredients carefully if you have any allergies, and, if in doubt, consult a health professional. Adult supervision is required for all recipes.

Introduction

Halloween is one of my favourite times of the year, and I'm super excited to take you on a spooky food adventure that is perfect for this wonderful season. Halloween is all about fun, creativity and family, and what better way to celebrate than by making some delicious and healthy treats together?

In this book, you'll find tons of easy and yummy recipes. Whether you're a little witch, wizard, mummy or monster, there's something for everyone. From fiendish party food and tasty tricks and treats to scary showstoppers, each recipe is simple to follow and good for you, too!

Cooking together is a fantastic way to make memories, learn new skills and have some fun. So, grab your aprons, wash those claws and let's get started on a Halloween cooking adventure you'll never forget.

Happy Halloween!

David

Contents

Tasty tricks and treats

Spooky showstoppers

Equipment list

Before you begin, it's a good idea to check what equipment you might need. Here is a list of the basic equipment you will use in this book, but check each recipe individually too.

Baking
paper

Baking
trays

Beaker

Biscuit
cutters

Child's
safety
knife

Cooling rack

Cupcake tray
(12-hole)

Digital scales

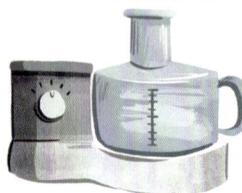
Food
processor

Frying pan

Glass bowl

Kitchen
scissors

Large mixing
bowl

Measuring
jug

Measuring
spoons

Muffin tray
(12-hole)

Oven
gloves

Oven
timer

Piping bags
and nozzles

Rolling
pin

Saucepan

Sandwich
bag

Spatula

Standard
cupcake cases

Stick
blender

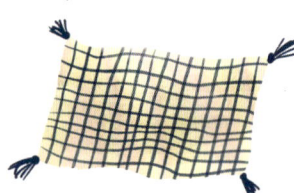
Tea towel

Whisk

Wooden
spoon

Wooden
lollipop sticks

Remember to always ask an adult to help when you're baking. And don't forget to wash and dry your hands!

FIENDISH PARTY FOOD

Ingredients

280ml warm water

50g spinach

40ml olive oil

400g strong white bread
  flour, plus extra for dusting

100g strong wholemeal
  bread flour

1 tsp fast-action yeast
  (1 sachet)

1 tsp table salt

12 almonds

2 tsp sesame seeds

Makes 12 breadsticks

Top tip: knead 100g grated cheese into your dough (at step 4). This gives a lovely flavour and will make the breadsticks look even more knobbly.

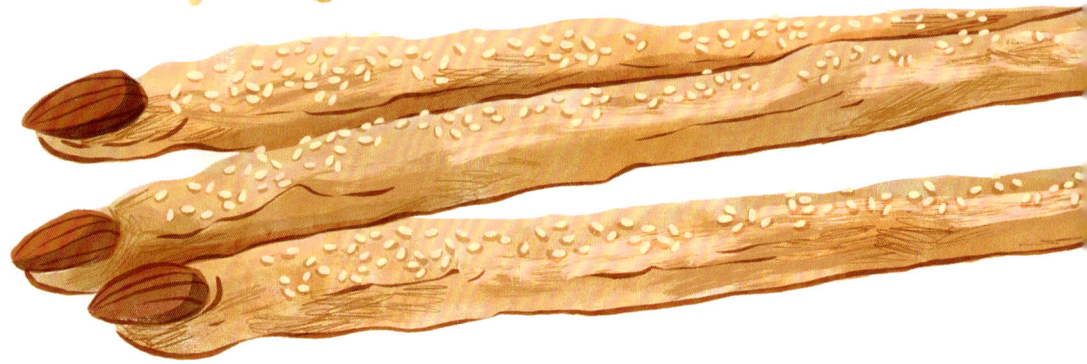

Witches' fingers breadsticks

I've never met a witch, but I imagine they have long, knobbly fingers, just like breadsticks. These fingers are perfect for dipping in your favourite sauce … or tickling your friends!

Method

1 Pour the warm water into a measuring jug. Add the spinach and oil, then whizz with a stick blender until smooth.

2 In a large mixing bowl, stir together the flours, yeast and salt, then pour in the green water. Mix until a sticky dough forms.

3 Cover and leave for 5 minutes.

4 Tip the dough out onto a lightly floured surface and knead for 3 minutes (do not add extra flour; it doesn't matter if it starts off sticky).

5 Return the dough to the bowl, cover and allow to rise in a warm place until it doubles in size (this will take more than an hour).

6 Tip the dough onto a lightly floured surface. Divide the dough in half, then cut each half into 6 pieces. Use both hands to roll each piece into a sausage shape that is 2cm in width, but no longer than your tray.

7 Line 2 large baking trays with baking paper and place the breadsticks onto the trays.

8 Press almonds firmly onto the end of each breadstick.

9 Cover and leave to rise in a warm place for 20 minutes.

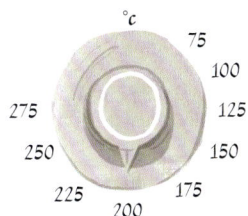

10 Preheat oven to 200°C (fan-assisted).

11 Brush with water, leave for 20 seconds, then sprinkle with sesame seeds.

12 Bake for 12 minutes. Allow to cool before serving.

Ingredients

350g self-raising flour,
  plus extra for dusting

1 tsp baking powder

2 tbsp poppy seeds

80g unsalted butter

165ml semi-skimmed milk,
  plus extra for brushing

25g basil leaves

1 tsp lemon juice

100g Cheddar cheese (diced
  into ½cm cubes)

100g feta cheese (crumbled)

Makes 12-14 scones

Zombie scones

These scones may look scary, but they taste delicious.
They are made out of green dough and cheesy chunks
that bubble when cooked. You can't let the zombies
escape, so once you've baked them, you need to make
sure all of them are eaten!

Method

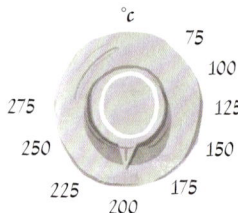

1 Preheat oven to
200°C (fan-assisted).

2 Line 2 large baking
trays with baking paper.

3 Put the flour, baking powder, poppy seeds and
butter into a mixing bowl. Rub the ingredients
together until the mixture looks like breadcrumbs.

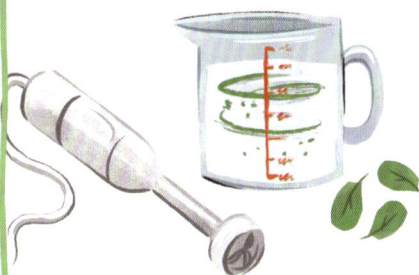

4 Put the milk, basil leaves and lemon juice into a measuring jug, and whizz with a stick blender until smooth.

5 Add the diced Cheddar cheese and crumbled feta cheese to the mixing bowl.

6 Pour the milk mixture into the bowl and bring together to form a dough (don't knead). If the mixture looks wet, sprinkle in a little flour.

7 Tip the dough out onto a lightly floured surface and roll it out until it is 1–2cm thick.

8 Cut out using a gingerbread person cutter, transfer to the lined baking trays and brush the tops with milk.

9 Bake for 12 minutes, until nicely golden. Allow to cool on a cooling rack. They're best eaten when still a little warm.

13

Ingredients

150g strong white bread flour,
plus extra for dusting

150g plain flour

½ tsp baking powder

200g cold, unsalted butter
(diced into 1cm cubes)

1 tsp purple food colour gel

140ml cold water

100g Cheddar cheese (grated)

50ml semi-skimmed milk

50g sesame seeds

Makes 18–20 cheesy wands

Crunchy cheesy wands

I've not managed to cast a spell with these crunchy cheesy wands yet, but maybe I haven't been using the right spells. It takes quite a bit of time (and magic) to make rough-puff pastry, but I promise that it is worth the wait!

Method

1 Put the flours and baking powder into a large mixing bowl and toss together. Add the butter cubes.

2 Mix the purple food gel with the water, then pour into the mixing bowl. Gently mix with a spatula, then gently knead to a dough (try not to squash the butter too much).

3 On a lightly floured surface, roll the dough out to 1cm thick, then fold in half. Wrap, put it on a plate and chill in the fridge for 30 minutes.

4 Roll the pastry out to 0.5cm thick. Fold it in half, roll out to 0.5cm thick, then fold in half again. Wrap, put it on a plate and place it back in the fridge for 30 minutes.

5 Repeat step 4 one more time.

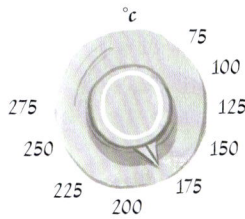

6 Preheat oven to 180°C (fan-assisted).

7 Line 2 large baking trays with baking paper.

8 On a lightly floured surface, roll the pastry out to 0.5cm thick, then sprinkle the grated cheese onto one half.

9 Fold the pastry over and roll it out again to make a rectangle shape that is about 20cm x 40cm and 0.5cm thick.

10 Cut the pastry into 18–20 lengths that are about 2cm wide.

11 Pour the milk into a little bowl. Tip the sesame seeds into another little bowl. Dip the end 3cm of each wand into the milk, then into the sesame seeds.

12 Place onto the baking trays and bake for 20 minutes until crisp and golden. Allow to cool before casting spells and eating.

Ingredients

Pizza dough:

400g strong white bread flour, plus extra for dusting

100g strong wholemeal bread flour

1 tsp fast-action yeast (1 sachet)

1 tsp table salt

300ml warm water

1 small carrot (peeled and finely grated)

Sauce:

1 tin chopped tomatoes

1 tsp dried oregano

½ tsp table salt

Toppings:

100g Red Leicester cheese (grated)

1 ball of mozzarella (cut into 8 slices)

50g tinned sweetcorn (drained)

16 green olive slices

Makes 8 mini pizzas

Monster face pizzas

Pizzas are my favourite dinner, and these mini pizzas are perfect for a party. Remember not to make them look *too* scary, otherwise people might be afraid to eat them!

Top tip: you can be as creative as you like, but use toppings that you would like to eat as that's the most important bit.

Method

1 In a large mixing bowl, combine the flours, yeast, salt, water and grated carrot until a sticky dough forms. Cover and leave to rest for 5 minutes.

2 Tip the dough onto a lightly floured surface and knead for 3 minutes (do not add extra flour; it doesn't matter if it starts off sticky).

3 Return the dough to the bowl, cover and allow to rise in a warm place until it doubles in size (this may take more than an hour).

4 While the dough is rising, tip the chopped tomatoes into a small saucepan with the oregano and salt. Simmer gently for 15 minutes, then leave to cool.

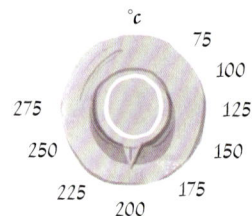

5 Preheat oven to 200ºC (fan-assisted).

6 Line 2 large baking trays with baking paper.

7 Tip the dough onto a lightly floured surface and divide into 8 pieces.

8 Roll into balls, then roll each ball out, with a rolling pin, until 0.5cm thick.

9 Add a spoonful of the sauce to each pizza and spread to the edges. Add some grated cheese and a slice of mozzarella for a mouth.

10 Add sweetcorn for the teeth and green olives for eyes.

11 Gently lift each pizza onto the baking trays.

12 Use scissors to snip around the edges of the pizzas to make hair.

13 Bake in the oven for 12–15 minutes until the cheese is bubbling. Allow to cool before eating.

Ingredients

40g frozen petit pois

1 garlic clove (peeled)

30g cashew nuts

40g Italian hard cheese

50ml olive oil, plus extra to
   drizzle over the pasta

½ tsp table salt

60g fresh basil (leaves and
   stalks, chopped)

250g wholewheat spaghetti

12 mozzarella pearls

12 green olive slices

Makes 6 servings

Serving suggestion: add some of the monster pizza sauce to the recipe for a yummy tomatoey kick.

Squirmy wormy pasta

One of my favourite stories when I was young was Roald Dahl's *The Twits*. In one scene, Mrs Twit serves Mr Twit worms instead of spaghetti. In this recipe we're not using real worms but spaghetti that *feels* like slippery, slidey worms and little mozzarella balls for eyeballs!

Method

1 Pour the peas into a bowl and ask an adult to help pour over a little boiling water, until the peas are covered.

2 Put the garlic, nuts and cheese into a food processor and whizz until the nuts are broken up.

3 Ask an adult to drain the peas, then tip them into the food processor. Add the oil, salt and chopped basil.

4 Pulse the pesto until smooth (but so you can still see little bits of basil).

5 With the help of an adult, simmer the pasta in boiling water for 10–12 minutes (or according to packet instructions).

6 Once the pasta is cooked, ask an adult to drain it. Add to a large mixing bowl. Drizzle over the oil and mix through.

7 Add the pesto and toss until the pasta is coated. Divide the wormy spaghetti between 6 bowls.

8 Add 2 mozzarella pearls, nestled in the middle of the wormy pasta. Place an olive slice on top of each pearl to make it look like an eyeball. Spooky!

Ingredients

Batter:

80g self-raising flour

½ tsp turmeric

80ml semi-skimmed milk

1 egg

4-5 tsps butter, for frying

Toppings:

100g hummus

1 small carrot (peeled and
  grated)

10 cherry tomatoes (halved)

Makes 8-10 pancakes

Petrified pancakes

When I make pancakes, I find it difficult to get them perfectly round. In this recipe, the more wibbly-wobbly the shapes, the better! These pancakes are soft and delicious, and you can add whatever toppings you like.

Method

1 Add the flour, turmeric and milk into a mixing bowl. Crack in the egg, then mix with a wooden spoon until smooth.

2 Allow to chill for 30 minutes in the fridge.

3 With the help of an adult, put the frying pan over a medium heat. When hot, add a little butter and, when melted, spoon in a ladle of pancake mixture.

4 When you see bubbles appear (after about 1 minute), ask your adult to flip and fry for another minute on the other side, then transfer to a plate.

5 Once all the pancakes are ready, cut out a mouth using a small, round biscuit cutter, then spread each with hummus.

6 Slice the pancake mouth in 2 and press onto the pancake to make ears. Add grated carrot for hair and tomato halves for eyes.

SWEET AND SCARY BAKES

Ingredients

Cupcakes:

2 Bramley apples (about 250g)
100ml vegetable oil
100g caster sugar
2 medium eggs
180g gluten-free plain flour
½ tsp ground mixed spice
1 tsp gluten-free baking
  powder

Toppings:

200g soft pitted dates
80g unsalted butter
30ml maple syrup
¼ tsp table salt

Makes 12 cupcakes

Toffee apple cupcakes

Gluten-free

Autumn is Halloween time, but it is also apple season. It is one of my favourite times of year because I love toffee apples. This bake isn't scary, spooky or kooky – it's a perfect October treat. And, what's better, these delicious cupcakes are gluten-free, so anyone who can't eat gluten can still tuck in!

Method

1 Ask an adult to peel, core and chop the apples into 1cm chunks. Put them in a bowl of cold water and set aside.

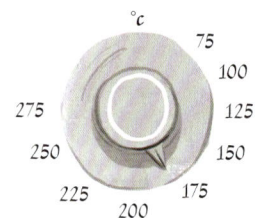

2 Preheat oven to 180°C (fan-assisted).

3 Prepare a 12-hole cupcake tray with 12 cupcake cases.

4 In a mixing bowl, beat together the oil and sugar. Crack the eggs into the bowl and beat until smooth.

5 Add the flour, mixed spice and baking powder and mix gently until just combined.

6 Drain the apples and stir the chunks through the mixture.

7 Fill the cupcake cases until three-quarters full. Bake for 20 minutes until golden brown, then leave to cool on a cooling rack.

Top tip: you need to use soft dates for this recipe. If your dates are not soft, ask an adult to soak them in hot water for 30 minutes, then drain.

8 Put the dates, butter, syrup and salt into a measuring jug and whizz with a stick blender until smooth.

9 If it looks too thick, ask an adult to add teaspoonfuls of boiling water, whizzing in between, until it is a spreadable consistency.

10 Once the cakes are cool, transfer the topping to a piping bag, snip off the end, then pipe a swirl on top of each cupcake.

Ingredients

Muffins:

140g frozen petit pois

100g plant-based spread

50ml dairy-free natural
  yogurt

2 medium eggs

120g caster sugar

1 tsp vanilla extract

1 tsp almond extract

180g self-raising flour

1 tsp baking powder

Decoration:

60g plant-based spread

200g icing sugar

60g strawberry jam

10 dairy-free white
  chocolate buttons

Makes 10 muffins

Monster muffins

Dairy-free

These monster muffins might look like they want to eat you, but don't worry: they can't bite. They are really soft and tasty, so you will want to gobble them up!

Top tip: make your monsters as colourful as you like. You can choose your own toppings for decoration.

Method

1 Put the frozen peas into a bowl, then ask an adult to pour over a little boiling water, until the peas are covered. Leave for 5 minutes.

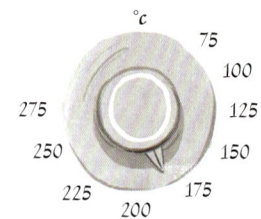

2 Preheat oven to 180°C (fan-assisted).

3 Put 10 cupcake cases into a 12-hole muffin tray.

4 Ask an adult to drain the peas. Add to a beaker with the butter, yogurt, eggs, sugar and extracts.

5 Whizz with a stick blender until smooth (this will take about 1 minute), then transfer to a mixing bowl.

6 Sieve in the flour and baking powder and mix with a wooden spoon until smooth.

7 Fill each cupcake case three-quarters full and bake for 15 minutes, or until the tops are springy to the touch.

8 While the cakes are cooling, beat together the butter and icing sugar.

9 Add the strawberry jam and beat until smooth, then transfer to a piping bag.

10 Remove the cakes from the paper cases and ask an adult to slice off the tops. Pipe a swirl of icing on each, then put the sliced tops back on and press down at one side.

11 Snap the chocolate buttons in half and use icing to stick two on top of each cake. Add another blob of icing for the centre of each eye.

Ingredients

Cupcakes:

2 ripe bananas (peeled)

100ml vegetable oil

¼ tsp grated nutmeg

50g caster sugar

50g soft brown sugar

120g self-raising flour

½ tsp baking powder

Decoration:

150g icing sugar

½ tsp vanilla extract

24 raisins

2 tbsp flaked almonds

Makes 12 cupcakes

Skull cupcakes

Dairy-free

Cupcakes are usually round, but with a clever trick we can make them skull-shaped. If you want to be very fancy, you can get some tubes of coloured icing and decorate your cakes with colourful patterns.

Top tip: it's important to use really ripe bananas for this recipe because they're soft and sweet. The best ones are brown or almost black.

Method

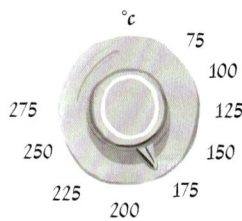

1 Preheat oven to 180°C (fan-assisted).

2 Fill a 12-hole cupcake tray with 12 cupcake cases.

3 Add the bananas, oil, nutmeg and sugars to a jug and whizz with a stick blender until smooth.

4 Pour the mixture into a mixing bowl. Add the flour and baking powder and mix until smooth (do not beat).

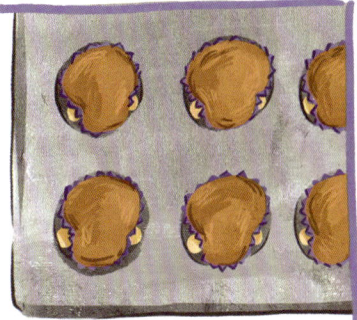

5 Fill each cupcake case three-quarters full. Gently push a baking bean (or scrunched-up ball of foil) either side of the case. Bake for 15 minutes, until golden.

6 For the icing, mix together the icing sugar and vanilla, then add a tablespoonful of water at a time until you have an icing that is pourable.

7 Dollop a spoonful of the icing onto the cake and spread to the edges.

8 Gently squeeze each raisin between your finger and thumb until soft, then place on the cakes for the eyes.

9 Break up the flaked almonds and add little pieces to each skull for the teeth.

Ingredients

Buns:

400g strong white bread
 flour, plus extra for dusting

100g strong wholemeal
 bread flour

1 tsp fast-action yeast
 (1 sachet)

1 tsp table salt

300ml warm water

1 small parsnip (peeled and
 finely grated)

Zest of 1 lemon

Decoration:

150g icing sugar

2–3 tsp lemon juice (from
 the zested lemon)

20g ground almonds

24 milk chocolate buttons

36 currants

Makes 10 iced buns

Iced mice buns

Lots of people find mice scary, but I think they're so cute! Even if your friends find real mice scary, they're going to love these tasty iced mice. Be warned though: these iced mice buns are a lot bigger than real mice!

Top tip: if you want to make brown mice or rat buns, add 50g cocoa powder at step 1 (reduce the amount of white flour to 350g) and use melted milk chocolate instead of icing to decorate.

Method

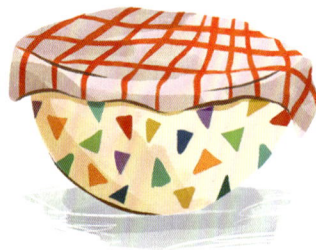

1 In a large mixing bowl, combine the flours, yeast, salt, water, parsnip and lemon zest until a sticky dough forms, then allow it to rest for 5 minutes.

2 Tip the dough out onto a lightly floured surface and knead for 3 minutes (do not add any extra flour; it doesn't matter if it starts off sticky).

3 Return the dough to the bowl, cover and leave it to rise in a warm place until it doubles in size (this will take over 1 hour).

4 Line 2 large baking trays with baking paper.

5 Tip the dough out and divide into 10 pieces.

6 Roll each piece into a ball, then, with the side of your hand, roll the end to a point. Set aside and leave to rest for 20 minutes.

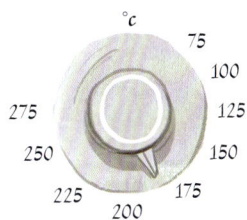

7 Preheat oven to 180°C (fan-assisted).

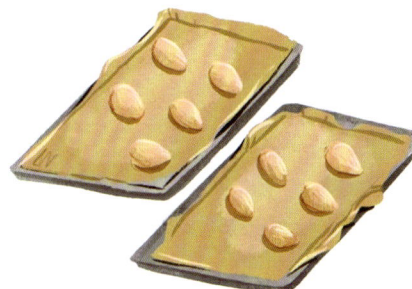

8 Transfer to the baking trays and bake for 12–14 minutes.

9 Beat together the icing sugar with the lemon juice (a teaspoonful at a time) until smooth and pourable.

10 Spread 1 spoonful of icing over each. Sprinkle on some ground almonds for fur, add 2 chocolate buttons for ears and press on 3 currants for the nose and eyes.

Sweet skeleton scones

Did you know that bones are very hard on the outside, but inside they're filled with bone marrow, which is soft? Scones are crunchy on the outside and very soft in the middle, so they're ideal to make tasty skeleton scones!

Ingredients

330g self-raising flour, plus extra for dusting

30g cocoa powder

1 tsp baking powder

50g caster sugar

60g plant-based spread

30g peanut butter

60g dairy-free milk chocolate chips

170ml dairy-free milk, plus extra for glazing

1 tsp vanilla extract

100g dairy-free white chocolate

Makes 8–10 scones

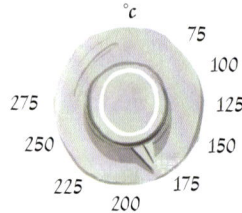

Method

1 Preheat oven to 180°C (fan-assisted).

2 Line 2 large baking trays with baking paper.

3 In a mixing bowl, rub together the flour, cocoa, baking powder, sugar, spread and peanut butter until it looks like breadcrumbs.

4 Toss through the chocolate chips.

5 Pour in the milk and vanilla, and mix until it forms a dough. Let it sit for 5 minutes.

6 Roll the dough out on a lightly floured surface until it is 1cm thick.

7 Cut out using a gingerbread person cutter and transfer them to the lined trays.

8 Brush the tops with milk and bake for 15 minutes. Leave to cool on a cooling rack.

9 Tip the white chocolate chips into a microwavable bowl. Ask an adult to microwave it for 30 seconds, then stir and repeat until the chocolate is melted and smooth.

10 Leave to cool slightly, then carefully transfer the white chocolate into a piping bag. Snip off the end and pipe on your skeleton design.

Spooky fact: there are 206 bones in the human body, but it'll be hard to pipe all these onto a skeleton scone. How many different bones can you add?

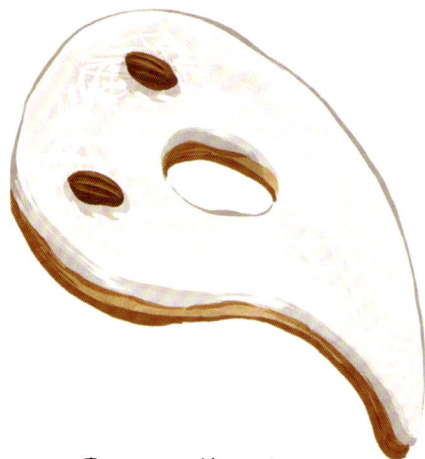

Ghost biscuits

These are clever cookies because each one starts out as a cute love-heart shape and then gets magically turned into two spooky, crunchy ghosts!

Ingredients

Biscuits:

75g unsalted butter

100g plain flour, plus extra for dusting

30g wholemeal plain flour

50g caster sugar

1 tsp vanilla extract

1 egg yolk

2 tsp water

Icing:

1 egg white

1 tsp vanilla extract

200g icing sugar

50g desiccated coconut

48 raisins

Makes 24 biscuits

Method

1 Line 2 large baking trays with baking paper.

2 Add the butter and flours to a food processor and blitz until you have fine crumbs. Add the sugar, vanilla, egg yolk and water and blitz again.

3 Tip the mixture out onto a lightly floured surface, then knead until you have a dough (don't knead too much after the dough has formed).

4 Wrap the dough and chill in the fridge for 30 minutes (perfect time to do a jigsaw).

5 On a lightly floured surface, roll out the dough until it is 0.5cm thick. Cut out the biscuits using a big heart-shaped cutter.

6 Ask an adult to use a knife to cut each biscuit in half, then place them on the baking trays.

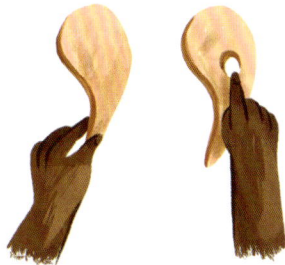

7 Using your fingers, curl the narrow tip of the biscuit to 1 side. Press a finger through the biscuit and wiggle to make the ghost's mouth.

8 Once you've filled the trays, place them in the fridge for 30 minutes.

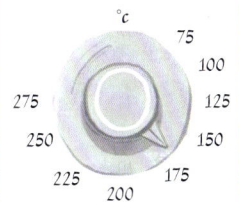

9 Preheat oven to 170°C (fan-assisted).

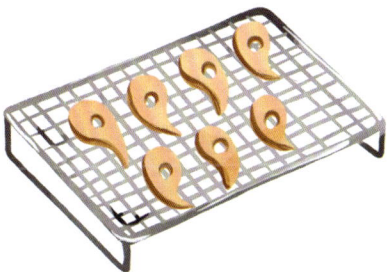

10 Bake the biscuits for 12–14 minutes, until golden, then cool on a cooling rack.

11 Beat together the egg white, vanilla and icing sugar until smooth. Tip the coconut onto a plate.

12 Once the biscuits are cool, spread over the icing, dip in the coconut and press on 2 raisins.

Ingredients

Whoopie pies:

120ml vegetable oil

180g soft brown sugar

1 medium egg

100g pumpkin purée (tinned)

250g plain flour

1 tsp baking powder

1 tsp ground cinnamon

½ tsp ground ginger

Filling:

80g unsalted butter (at room temperature)

150g icing sugar

1 tsp vanilla extract

80g full-fat cream cheese

Decoration:

Black cake pen

Makes 10–12 whoopie pies

Pumpkin whoopie pies

Every year I like to carve a pumpkin for Halloween, but I also like to eat cooked pumpkin as it's sweet, soft and delicious. You can bake these whoopie pies, then eat them as a special treat while carving your Halloween pumpkin.

Top tip: you can buy pumpkin purée in a tin, or make your own by roasting a pumpkin then blending the flesh until smooth.

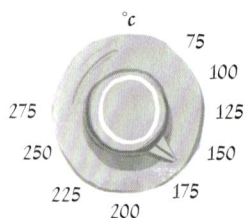

Method

1 Preheat oven to 170°C (fan-assisted).

2 Line 2 large baking trays with baking paper.

3 Beat together the oil, sugar and egg. Add the pumpkin purée and beat again until smooth.

4 Add the flour, baking powder and spices, then mix until just combined (be careful not to over-mix).

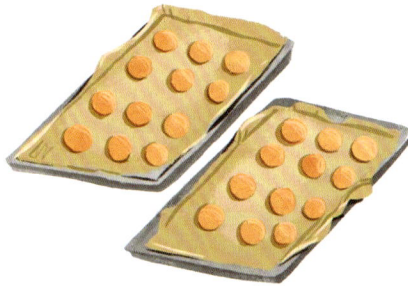

5 Spoon 10–12 blobs of mixture (about 5cm in diameter) onto each tray, leaving at least 2cm between each blob.

6 Bake for 12–14 minutes, until golden brown at the edges, then allow to cool.

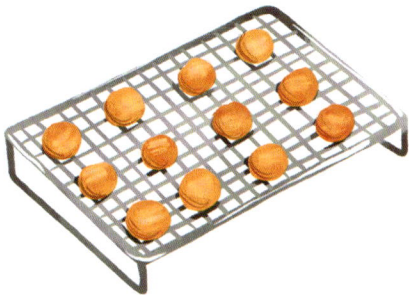

7 Once cool, use a spatula to lift each disc off the tray and onto a cooling rack.

8 For the filling, beat the butter until light and creamy. Add the icing sugar and beat until smooth.

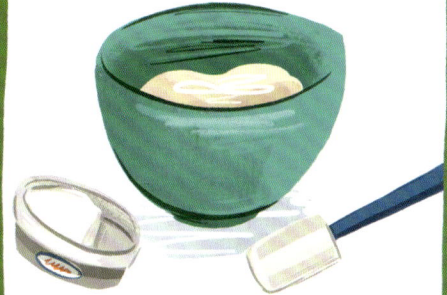

9 Finally add the vanilla and cream cheese and beat again.

10 Dollop a teaspoonful of filling onto 1 disc, sandwich with another and squeeze until the filling reaches the edges.

11 To decorate, use a black cake pen to draw a spooky face on your pumpkin whoopie pies. You could draw a different face for each pumpkin.

Ingredients

Cupcakes:

50g soft pitted dates

50ml boiling water

70ml vegetable oil

70g carrot (peeled and finely grated)

70g caster sugar

85g plain flour

15g cocoa powder

1 ½ tsp baking powder

Custard:

250ml oat milk

20g cornflour

25g caster sugar

½ tsp vanilla extract

½ tsp green food colour gel

16 gummy worms

Makes 8 puddings

Spooky swamp cups

Dairy-free

You never know what creepy crawlies, snakes, crocodiles or even monsters are hiding in a swamp. These spooky-looking swamp puddings with surprise gummy worms are a fun dessert to serve to your friends.

Method

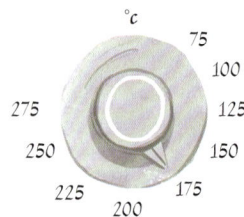

1 Preheat oven to 180°C (fan-assisted).

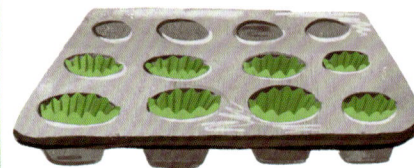

2 Prepare a 12-hole cupcake tray with 8 cupcake cases.

3 Add the dates to a measuring jug with the boiling water. Leave for 5 minutes, then pour in the oil and whizz with a stick blender until smooth.

4 Transfer to a mixing bowl with all the other cupcake ingredients and mix until smooth.

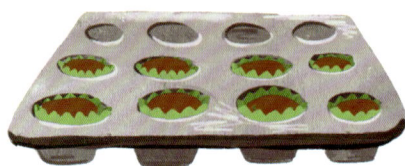

5 Fill each cupcake case three-quarters full, then bake for 12–15 minutes. Leave to cool on a cooling rack.

6 To make the custard, whisk together the oat milk, cornflour, sugar, vanilla and food gel. Stir over a medium heat continually until it thickens, then leave to cool.

7 Pour the custard halfway up 8 small cups. Crumble 1 cake over the top of each cup, then wiggle in 2 gummy worms.

TASTY TRICKS AND TREATS

Ingredients

3 bananas

100ml natural live yogurt

20g icing sugar

½ tsp vanilla extract

18 milk chocolate chips

Makes 6 lollies

Banana ghost pops

This treat is so, so simple and so tasty (as long as you like bananas). Bananas are different from lots of other fruits because they're not juicy. This means that when they freeze, they go creamy like ice cream. Yum!

Method

1 Peel the bananas and chop them in half widthways.

2 Push a lolly stick through the cut end of each half, until it reaches halfway.

3 Line a small baking tray with baking paper.

4 Mix the yogurt, icing sugar and vanilla together in a beaker or measuring jug.

Top tip: sprinkle desiccated coconut on top of your banana ghost pops (at step 6) for an extra tasty twist.

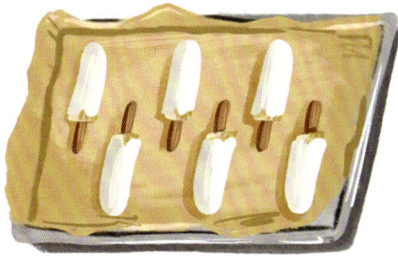

5 Dip the banana halves into the yogurt mixture and place on the lined tray.

6 Press on 2 chocolate drops for the eyes and 1 for the mouth.

7 Transfer to the freezer and freeze for at least 2 hours before eating.

Fizzy fudge stars

Is this a trick or a treat? This fudge is delicious, but the popping candy makes your mouth crackle and pop, which I love, but for others it's a bit of a surprise! This recipe uses halva, which is a sweet, tasty treat from the Middle East made from sesame and sugar.

Ingredients

200g milk chocolate

160g light tahini (stirred)

½ tsp vanilla extract

150g halva

2 small packets of
  popping candy

Makes 12-14 fudge stars

Method

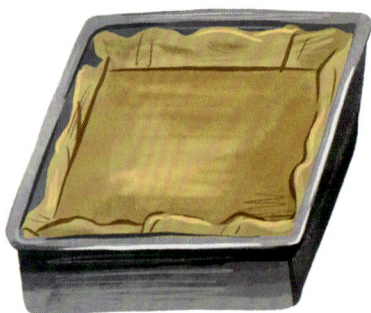

1 Line a 20cm square baking tin with baking paper, or cling film.

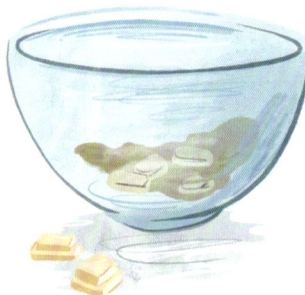

2 Put the chocolate, tahini and vanilla extract into a heatproof bowl and stir together.

3 Ask an adult to help you place the bowl on top of a saucepan of simmering water and stir until smooth.

4 Crumble in the halva, stir it through, then ask an adult to pour the mixture into the tin. Press it into the sides with a spoon.

5 Sprinkle over the popping candy and allow to cool to room temperature.

6 Transfer to the fridge and chill for 2 hours.

Top tip: if you can't find halva, you can use nougat instead.

7 Remove the fudge from the tin and, using a star biscuit cutter, cut out as many stars as you can.

8 Save the stars for the trick-or-treaters, but the offcuts are for you!

Fruity snake tongues

Dairy-free

Fruit leather is sweet and chewy, but it is made purely of fruit, so it is also the perfect healthy snack to give out to trick-or-treaters. Unroll your fruity tongue and hang it out of your mouth to spook your friends and family!

Ingredients

350g frozen strawberries (defrosted)

5 soft pitted dates

20g chia seeds

Makes 10 fruity rolls

Method

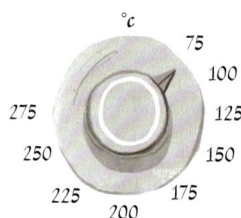

1 Preheat oven to 80°C (fan-assisted).

2 Line 2 medium-sized baking trays (about 30cm x 20cm) with baking paper.

3 Put the strawberries and dates into a blender and whizz until smooth.

4 Add to a saucepan and simmer gently for 10–15 minutes until thick (you should be able to see the bottom of the pan if you pull a spoon through the mixture).

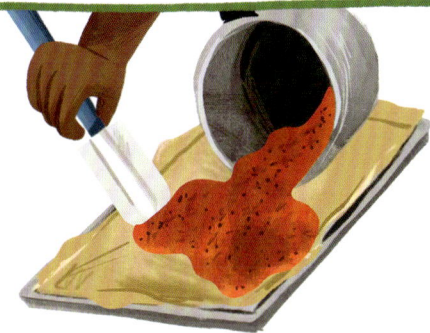

5 Stir through the chia seeds, then pour the mixture onto the lined trays (it should be about 0.3cm thick). Make sure to spread it to the edges (it should be a bit thicker at the sides, as the edges dry first).

6 Put the tray in the oven and bake for 6 hours. Make your trick-or-treating outfit while you're waiting!

7 When the leather is ready, it'll be shiny and dry, but not sticky to touch.

8 Cut each fruit sheet into 5 strips (lengthways) that are about 4cm wide and roll up tightly.

9 Cut a triangle out of the end to make a fork in the tongue.

Ingredients

100g sweet biscuits

60g assorted nuts

20g raisins

20g dried cranberries

20g dried apricots (chopped)

150g milk chocolate

50ml runny honey

60g peanut butter

100ml Greek yogurt

Makes 10-12 tiffin bites

Mini tiffin mummies

One day I made a big batch of tiffin and decided to freeze some for the next week. When I took it out of the freezer, I was too impatient to let it defrost, and I realized that tiffin is delicious when frozen! This gave me the idea to make tiffin mummies, with piped frozen yogurt for the bandages.

Top tip: this recipe uses a mini gingerbread person cutter, but you can use any mini cutter you like.

Method

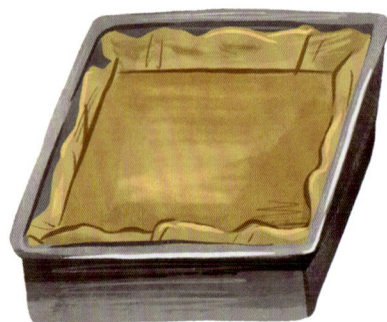

1 Line a 20cm square baking tin with baking paper.

2 Put the biscuits into a sandwich bag. Bash them with the end of a rolling pin until you have lots of small pieces (about 1cm big).

3 Put the nuts into a food processor and blitz. If you don't have a food processor, tip into a sandwich bag and bash them with the end of a rolling pin until you have a fine powder.

4 Mix the biscuit crumbs and nuts with the raisins, cranberries and apricots.

5 Break the chocolate into a saucepan. Add the honey and peanut butter, then ask an adult to help you stir the mixture over a medium heat until melted.

6 Tip the dry mixture into the chocolatey mixture and stir until combined.

7 Spoon the mixture into the tin, then press flat with the back of the spoon.

8 Chill in the fridge for 1 hour.

9 Lift the tiffin out of the tin using the baking paper and place on a work surface. Leave for 30 minutes, until it has softened a little but is still set.

10 Ask an adult to cut out the tiffin with a biscuit cutter (they will need to press down hard and wiggle the cutter).

11 Fill a piping bag with the yogurt. Snip off the end of the bag, then pipe squiggles over each piece of tiffin.

12 Place the tiffin back on a baking tray and freeze for at least 1 hour before eating.

Iced skull cookies

You can cleverly use a circular biscuit cutter to make these spooky skull-shaped cookies. Yum!

Method

Ingredients

Cookies:

200g unsalted butter
  (at room temperature)

50g caster sugar

50ml runny honey

200g plain flour

50g ground almonds

Decoration:

125g icing sugar

Orange food colour gel

Red food colour gel

Green food colour gel

40 raisins

20g flaked almonds

Makes 18-20 cookies

1 In a mixing bowl, beat together the butter, sugar and honey until smooth.

2 Add the flour and ground almonds and bring together until you have a dough (do not over-mix).

3 Allow to chill for 30 minutes in the fridge.

4 Preheat oven to 160°C (fan-assisted).

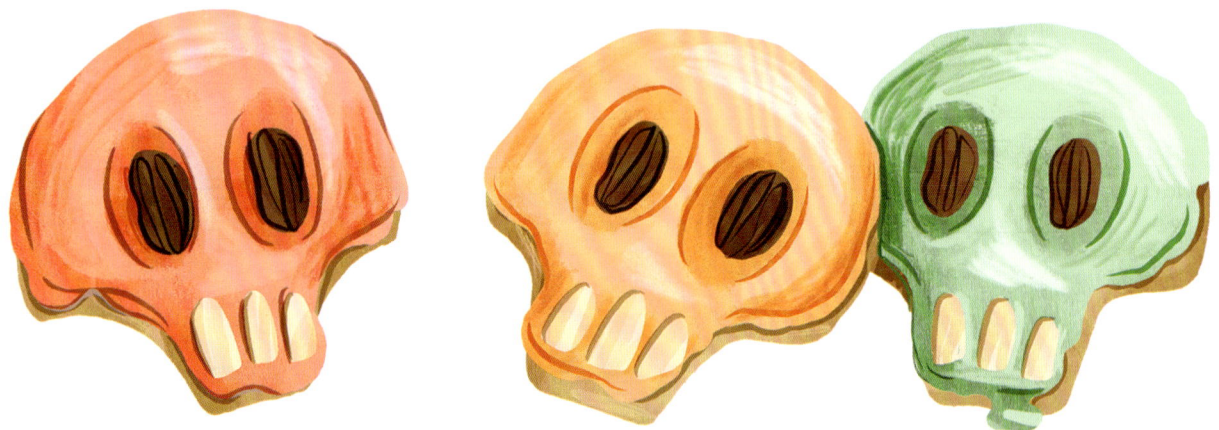

5 Line 2 large baking trays with baking paper.

6 On a lightly floured surface, roll out the dough to 0.5cm thick.

7 Use a round cutter to cut out each biscuit. Then, using the cutter, remove a section on either side to make a skull shape.

8 Transfer the biscuits to a baking tray and use your fingers to create 2 eye sockets.

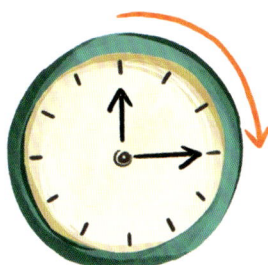

9 Bake for 12–15 minutes, until golden at the edges, then leave to cool.

10 Tip the icing sugar into a bowl and mix in teaspoonfuls of water, until you have a pourable icing.

11 Divide the icing between 3 bowls, adding a couple of drops of food gel to each.

12 Dip a cooled cookie into your chosen coloured icing and leave it to set. Continue until you have lots of colourful iced skull cookies!

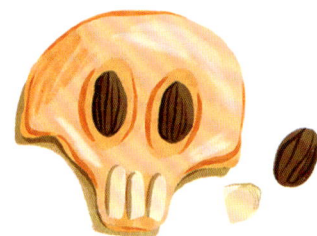

13 Add raisins for the eyes. Break up flaked almonds into little pieces for the teeth.

Ingredients

2 medium eggs

120g caster sugar

1 tsp white wine vinegar

30 colourful chocolate sweets

30 milk chocolate chips

Makes about 30
mini meringues

Meringue eyeballs

I've never eaten an eyeball before, but I think they would be slimy and slippery. These meringue eyeballs may look like the real thing, but don't worry, they are deliciously crunchy and sweet.

Method

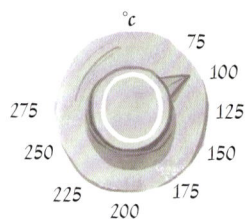

1 Preheat oven to 100°C (fan-assisted).

2 Line 2 large baking trays with baking paper.

3 Ask an adult to help you crack the eggs, one at a time, into your hands over a mixing bowl. Let the whites slip through your fingers. Drop the yolks into another bowl.

4 Whisk the egg whites with an electric mixer until fluffy, then add the sugar, a little at a time, and the vinegar until the mixture is shiny and glossy.

5 Add the mixture to a piping bag. Snip off the end to make an opening that is about 0.5cm wide. If you don't have a piping bag, use a sandwich bag with the end cut off.

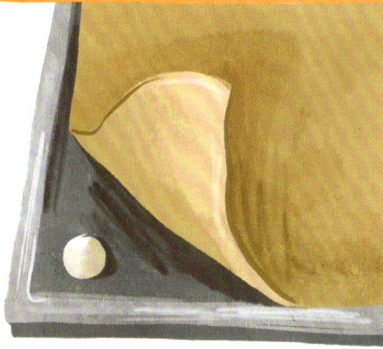

6 Put a little blob of mixture in each corner of the baking trays and stick the baking paper down.

7 Pipe 15 blobs of meringue (about 4cm in diameter) onto each tray, holding the tip 1cm above the tray as you squeeze. Do not lift the piping bag up until you've finished piping, so that you get a blob rather than a peak.

8 Gently push a sweet onto each eyeball and bake for 1 hour. Leave to cool a little.

9 Push a chocolate chip on top of each sweet while they're still a bit warm (this will stick it on).

Ingredients

100g dark chocolate

100g milk chocolate

100g white chocolate

Green food gel

A handful of nuts, dried fruit
  and Halloween sprinkles (or
  colourful sweets)

Makes 12-14 servings

Magical chocolate bark

Here is a fun way to use the treats collected from your Halloween adventures. You can add all kinds of toppings to your chocolate bark, then break it into lots of colourful pieces to share.

Method

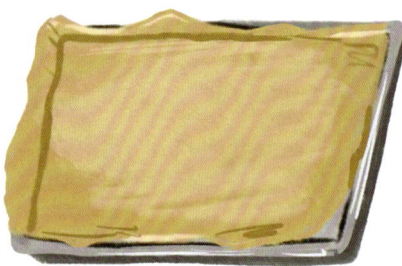

1 Line a medium-sized baking tray with baking paper.

2 Break your dark chocolate into pieces and put them in a microwavable jug.

3 Ask an adult to melt the chocolate in the microwave by heating it for 30 seconds and stirring. Repeat this step until the chocolate has melted.

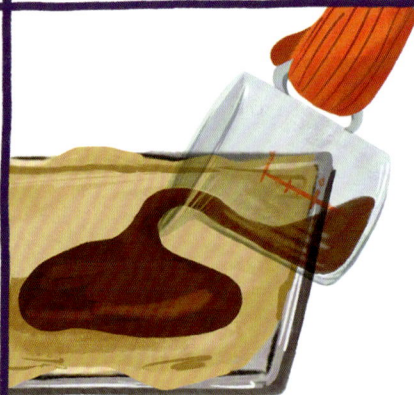

4 Pour the melted chocolate onto the baking tray, making sure to spread it to the edges.

5 Repeat steps 2 and 3 with the milk chocolate and pour it on top of the dark chocolate, using a blunt knife to swirl it around.

6 Ask an adult to melt the white chocolate in the microwave, then add a couple of drops of green food gel. Stir in the gel until the chocolate goes green, then leave to cool a little.

7 Once cooler, use a spoon to drop splodges of green chocolate onto the swirled chocolate.

8 Sprinkle over your chosen toppings as quickly as you can to make sure they stick before the chocolate sets.

9 Leave to cool, then place the tray in the fridge for at least 2 hours.

10 Once set, use the end of a rolling pin to break the chocolate slab into pieces.

Ingredients

100g puffed rice cereal

100g milk chocolate

100g soft pitted dates

30g raisins

100g porridge oats

A handful of Halloween
  sprinkles (or colourful sweets)

Makes 12-14 treats

Black cat litter tray

This is a really fun and cheeky trick to play on your trick-or-treaters. They might think you're offering them cat poo, but they'll actually get a yummy chocolatey treat. Phew!

Method

1 Pour the puffed rice onto a small baking tray.

2 Ask an adult to melt the chocolate in the microwave for 30 seconds at a time, stirring until the chocolate is just melted.

3 Ask an adult to roughly chop the dates and raisins until you have smaller chunks.

4 Add the chopped fruit and oats to the melted chocolate and stir with a wooden spoon until smooth.

5 Take a teaspoonful of mixture and roll it in your hands until you have a small ball shape. Place it on top of the puffed rice.

6 Place the chocolate treats on top of the puffed rice, then sprinkle on some Halloween sprinkles or sweeties to add extra colour.

SPOOKY SHOWSTOPPERS

Ingredients

135g orange jelly blocks

150g blueberries

1 apple (peeled, cored and cut
  into thin circular slices)

1 tsp lemon juice

135g lime jelly blocks

50g chia seeds

135g lemon jelly blocks

6 green, seedless grapes
  (halved lengthways)

Makes 8-10 servings

Pond pudding

When I was a kid, the slimiest thing I ever touched was frogspawn. Chia seeds are a delicious and healthy seed, and when you put them in water, a really cool thing happens - they become soft and slimy, just like frogspawn! This is a fun and colourful dessert, with blueberries as rocks at the bottom of your pond, apple slices as lily pads, and chia seed jelly as frogspawn.

Method

1 Ask an adult to pour 300ml of boiling water into a measuring jug. Break the orange jelly into cubes and carefully add them to the jug. Stir until all the jelly has dissolved.

2 Add 200ml of cold water, stir well, then pour into a big glass bowl.

3 Drop the blueberries into the orange jelly, then put in the fridge for 1-2 hours.

4 Use the end of a heart cutter to press out a notch in each apple slice to make lily pads. Add to a bowl of water mixed with lemon juice until ready to use.

5 To make the lime jelly, follow steps 1–2, but add the apple slices after pouring the jelly onto the set orange jelly (keep 2–3 back for decoration). Return to the fridge for 1–2 hours to set.

Top tip: if you want to change the fruits be careful not to use pineapple, kiwi or papaya as these will stop the jelly setting.

6 Add the chia seeds to a bowl with 200ml of cold water. Leave them for at least 20 minutes.

7 Drain the chia seeds. Make the lemon jelly (follow steps 1–3) and stir the chai seeds through it before pouring on top of the set lime jelly.

8 Place in the fridge for a final 2-hour chill.

9 When the jelly has set, decorate the top of the jelly with the remaining apple slices. Add grape halves, to make bubbles on top of the jelly pond.

Pumpkin patch brownies

Each year I love going to pick a pumpkin from our local pumpkin patch. There is a chocolate cake called "chocolate mud cake", which made me think that chocolate brownies would make a gooey and delicious base for a cute and edible pumpkin patch.

Ingredients

Brownies:

100ml vegetable oil

200g caster sugar

1 tsp vanilla extract

190g plain flour

30g wholemeal plain flour

30g cocoa powder

2 tsp baking powder

¼ tsp table salt

250g courgette (finely grated)

60g milk chocolate chips

Toppings:

80g ground almonds

60g icing sugar

15ml water

½ tsp almond extract

Orange food colour gel

Green food colour gel

100g milk chocolate

Makes 12 servings

Method

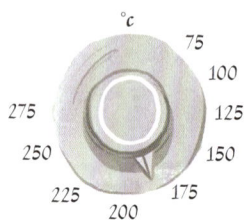

1 Preheat oven to 180°C (fan-assisted).

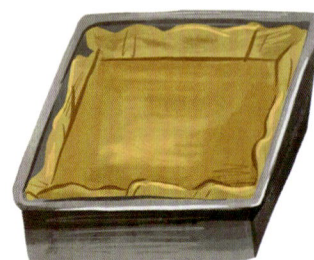

2 Grease a 20cm square tin and line with baking paper.

3 Put the oil, sugar, vanilla, flours, cocoa, baking powder and salt into a mixing bowl. Rub together until it looks like a crumble mixture.

4 Add the grated courgette and chocolate chips and gently stir until combined. Allow to sit for 5 minutes.

5 Stir the mixture again and pour it into the baking tin.

6 Bake for 25–30 minutes (the middle should still be a little soft).

7 To make the pumpkins, combine the ground almonds, icing sugar, water and almond extract. Knead until you have a smooth dough (if it feels coarse, add 1 tsp of extra water).

8 Split the dough into 3. Push 2 of the pieces back together, then knead in a few drops of orange gel. Add a few drops of green gel to the remaining piece and knead.

9 Roll 6 balls from the orange dough. Use the edge of a spoon to create the ridges of a pumpkin.

10 Divide the green marzipan into 2. Roll 1 half into a long, thin sausage shape to make the vines. Make little balls out of the other half, flattening them with your thumb and finger to create leaves.

11 Once the brownie is baked, ask an adult to remove it from the tin and trim about 0.5cm off the edges. Crumble the edges into a bowl.

12 Ask your adult to melt the chocolate in the microwave for 30 seconds, then stir and repeat until the chocolate is melted and smooth.

13 Add half the cake crumbs, mix then spoon the chocolate over the brownie. Sprinkle more cake crumbs on top.

14 Arrange the pumpkins, vines and leaves to make your pumpkin patch.

Ingredients

280g plain flour, plus extra
  for dusting

50g ground almonds

50g caster sugar

190g unsalted butter

1 egg

1 tsp cold water

400g frozen summer fruits
  (defrosted and drained)

15g cornflour

30g caster sugar, plus extra
  for sprinkling

Makes 10–12 servings

Vampire fruit pie

When you're making a fruit pie, the juices from the inside can bubble through the top and people often think this looks untidy. For this pie, you don't need to worry, as it's meant to happen and adds to the spookiness!

Method

1 Put the flour, ground almonds, sugar and butter into a food processor and blitz until you have fine crumbs.

2 Crack the egg over a small bowl and let the egg white fall through your fingers while containing the yolk in your hand.

3 Add the yolk and cold water to the food processor and blitz again until combined.

4 Tip the mixture onto a lightly floured surface and squish it with your hands until you have a dough (do not knead).

5 Wrap the dough and put it in the fridge to chill for 30 minutes.

6 Mix the fruits with the cornflour and sugar and set aside.

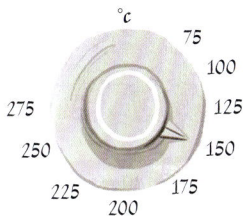

7 Preheat the oven to 150°C (fan-assisted).

8 Take two thirds of the pastry and roll out on a lightly floured surface until it is 0.5cm thick.

9 Gently lift the pastry onto the pie dish and push down into the corners. Trim the edges, leaving about 0.5cm over the top of the dish.

10 Cover with baking paper, fill with baking beans and bake for 18–20 minutes.

11 Ask an adult to take it out of the oven, remove the paper and baking beans, and then return it to the oven for another 5 minutes.

12 Roll out the remaining third of pastry to 0.5cm thick. Cut out a mouth and 2 eyes using a safety knife or biscuit cutters. Put the offcuts to one side.

13 Tip the fruit mix into the pie crust, spread it evenly and then gently add the pie top. Push down the edges, then, using the offcuts, make vampire teeth, eyebrows and other decorations.

14 Brush the top with the egg white, add your extra decorations, then sprinkle with sugar. Bake for 40 minutes until golden brown and bubbling.

Ingredients

Cake:

1 banana (peeled)

75ml vegetable oil

30g spinach

100ml natural live yogurt

1 tsp vanilla extract

1 medium egg

120g plain flour

50g wholemeal plain flour

140g caster sugar

½ tsp baking powder

½ tsp bicarbonate of soda

Decoration:

150g unsalted butter (at room temperature)

120g icing sugar

15ml boiling water

Green food colour gel

4 marshmallows

40g milk chocolate

Makes 10-12 servings

Frankenstein cake

This cake looks brilliant but is very easy to make and decorate. The cake isn't just green on the outside; it's also green on the inside because there is spinach in the cake batter. You can decorate your Frankenstein's monster cake any way you wish. You could even add your trick-or-treat sweets to the top of the cake.

Method

1. Preheat oven to 160°C (fan-assisted).

2. Line a 20cm square tin with baking paper.

3. Put the banana, oil, spinach, yogurt, vanilla and egg into a mixing bowl and whizz with a hand blender until smooth.

4. In a separate bowl, toss together the flours, sugar, baking powder and bicarbonate of soda.

5 Pour in the wet ingredients and mix until just combined (don't beat).

6 Pour into the tin and bake for 30–35 minutes (or until a skewer comes out clean). Leave to cool.

7 Ask an adult to transfer the cake to a cake board. Slice 2cm from one side of the cake. Cut this offcut into 3 pieces and arrange them to make the neck.

8 To make the buttercream, beat the butter until smooth.

9 Tip the icing sugar into a separate bowl. Ask an adult to pour in the boiling water and add 3–4 drops of green food gel. Add to the butter and beat until smooth.

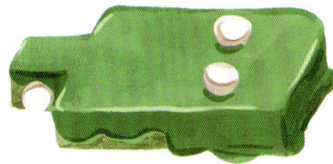

10 Spread the buttercream over the tops and sides of the cake, then add 2 marshmallows for eyes, and 2 marshmallows for the neck bolts.

11 Break the chocolate into a microwavable bowl. Ask an adult to heat it for 30 seconds, then stir and repeat until melted.

12 Transfer the cooled chocolate into a piping bag. Snip off the end, dot on eyes then pipe your design.

David Atherton was the winner of *The Great British Bake Off* 2019. David's cookery books for children – *My First Cook Book: Bake, Make and Learn to Cook*; *My First Green Cook Book: Vegetarian Recipes for Young Cooks* and *My First Baking Book: Delicious Recipes for Budding Bakers* – inspired a generation of children to create healthy, imaginative recipes for their friends and family. David is a food writer and an international health adviser for a charity. He has worked on health programmes around the world and never misses an opportunity to explore a new food culture. David is passionate about ensuring that children grow up as food lovers and understand how to make tasty, healthy food.

Jess Rose is an illustrator, designer and author. As a digital illustrator, Jess gives the effects of hand-applied techniques to her work, such as paint marks, ink and print qualities, and creates impactful, bright illustrations. Jess's own picture books include *No Home for a Ghost* and *Fantastic Frankie*. Her illustrated picture books include *Dilwyn the Welsh Dragon*, which was read on *CBeebies Bedtime Stories* and *Two Places to Call Home* and *Two Families to Call My Own*, written by Phil Earle.